GARTH BROOKS

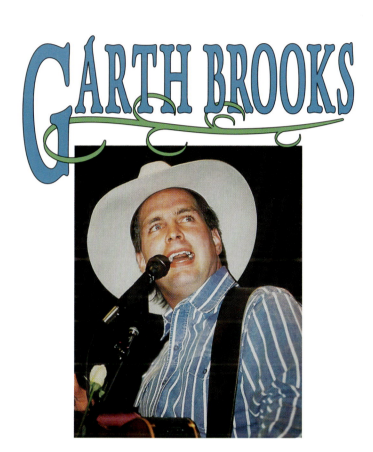

CHART-BUSTIN' COUNTRY

Paul Howey

Lerner Publications Company ● Minneapolis

To my mom, who always wanted an author for a son—
or was it the other way around?

This book is available in two bindings:
Library binding by Lerner Publications Company
Soft cover by First Avenue Editions
241 First Avenue North
Minneapolis, MN 55401

Website address: www.lernerbooks.com

LIBRARY OF CONGRESS CATALOGING-IN-PUBLICATION DATA

Howey, Paul M.
  Garth Brooks : chart bustin' country / Paul M. Howey.
     p.   cm.
  Includes index.
  Summary: Follows the life and work of the popular singer-
songwriter who went from struggling musician to multimillionaire.
  ISBN 0–8225–2898–3 (lib. bdg.)
  ISBN 0–8225–9809–4 (pbk.)
  1. Brooks, Garth—Juvenile literature. 2. Country musicians—
United States—Biography—Juvenile literature. 3. Brooks, Garth.
[1. Musicians. 2. Country music.] I. Title.
ML3930.B855H69   1998
782.421642'092—dc21
[B]   97–6888

Manufactured in the United States of America
1 2 3 4 5 6 – JR – 03 02 01 00 99 98

Contents

Introduction

Garth Brooks didn't last even one day in Nashville, Tennessee. He had driven there from Stillwater, Oklahoma, in 1985, expecting the nation's music capital to roll out the red carpet for him. "I thought you'd go there, flip open your guitar case, play a song, and someone would hand you a million bucks," he later recalled. Even if Nashville *had* been ready for him, Garth wasn't ready for Nashville.

Throughout the day, he walked up and down the streets of Nashville, knocking on the doors of some of the most important people in the recording industry. That was the easy part. Getting the doors to open, however, was quite another matter.

That afternoon, he finally did get to meet with an executive at the American Society of Composers,

Authors, and Publishers (ASCAP). Their meeting was interrupted by a songwriter who came into the room and asked to borrow $500 from the executive. The ASCAP executive flatly turned down the songwriter's request.

Surprised, Garth remarked that he made more than $500 a week singing in bars back home. "Then I'd advise you to go back home," the executive told him. "You've got your choices. You either starve as a songwriter or get five people together and go out and starve as a band."

That piece of advice was more than Garth could take. He retreated to his motel room and stared through the window at the rain. Stung by the swirling emotions of rejection, anger, panic, and humiliation, he impulsively grabbed his bags, got in his car, and headed home.

Neither Garth nor the ASCAP executive could possibly have imagined that in just a few short years, this struggling musician would be a multimillionaire. His face would be on the cover of nearly every major magazine, and he would be one of the most successful recording artists in history.

Garth Brooks with his parents, Colleen and Troyal

A Blended Family

Troyal Garth Brooks was born on February 7, 1962, in Tulsa, Oklahoma. A few years later, his family moved to Yukon, a small town of about 20,000 people located just west of Oklahoma City. Yukon, which calls itself "one of America's safest cities," is a quiet town overlooking the North Canadian River bottomlands.

The Brookses were both an extended and a blended family. Each of Garth's parents had been married once before. His father, Troyal Raymond Brooks, had one child by his previous marriage. His

Garth, *right,* was the quarterback on the Yukon High School football team. He is shown here going over some plays with head coach, Milt Bassett.

mother, Colleen Carroll Brooks, had three. Together, Troyal and Colleen had two more children—Kelly and, 18 months later, Garth.

The family made a strong point of stating they had no stepchildren and the children had no half brothers or sisters. They were a single family unit and would fight anyone in town who said otherwise.

Garth's mother was a featured singer on Red Foley's *Ozark Jubilee,* a weekly radio and television show in the 1950s. Between 1955 and 1957, she recorded four singles for Capitol Records, but eventually she gave up her singing career to be a full-time mother. Garth's father, a former marine, worked for more than 30 years as an engineer and draftsman for an oil company. He was an intimidating yet gentle father figure.

Garth's parents recognized the value of knowledge and insisted that education come before nearly everything else in their children's lives. Though Troyal never made more than $25,000 a year, all six of the Brooks

The Brookses' family home in Yukon, Oklahoma, was filled with love, laughter, and music.

children went to college, and all but one—Garth's sister, Betsy—graduated.

The Brookses' split-level brick home at 408 Yukon Avenue was a center of love and support for the children. Troyal once said that "the kids were just as much a part of what went on in that house as Colleen and I were."

Garth describes his parents, saying, "My dad was a cool guy. . . . He pretty much cut straight to it. And Mom could make the worst things sound great. They were a great pair, because they'd level each other out. One was an extreme realist, one was an extreme dreamer. And both were extreme doers." Garth says of his father, "If I could be like any man in the world, it would be him."

In his junior year, Garth, *standing third from left,* played on the Yukon baseball team.

Holidays were especially festive events in the Brooks household. During Easter egg hunts, Troyal and Colleen taped coins to the eggs—as an added incentive—and later switched to dollar bills as the children grew older. At Halloween, Colleen often dressed as a witch, stood outside the house, and gave candy to people passing by. Decorating for Christmas began the day after Thanksgiving.

Children were always around—sometimes more than 150 of them after high school pep rallies. Colleen said nothing was ever really damaged—that is until Betsy's 16th birthday. By the time the all-girl party was over, two steps were broken, a hole somehow "appeared" in a wall, and jelly beans and icing were stuck to the ceiling.

The Brookses' home was also a house of music. Several family members played guitars and sang, and they provided a ready-made audience if anyone wanted to perform. "Funny Night" was a weekly event. Family members sang, did imitations, and acted in skits. Troyal played the guitar—as did Jerry, Mike, and Betsy. Jim played the harmonica, and Garth, his musical talent not yet developed, played the wax comb with brother Kelly. Betsy recalls that her youngest brother began participating in Funny Night when he was only two years old. "Garth would want right in the middle of it, and he'd capture your attention," she said.

The music of singer
George Strait had a
strong influence on
Garth.

As he grew up, Garth liked a wide variety of music,
including that by James Taylor, Dan Fogelberg, George
Jones, and Merle Haggard. As a teenager, he liked
hard rock groups, such as Kiss and Queen. Their concerts later shaped Garth's own explosive performance
style. But not until he heard George Strait's "Un-
wound" in 1980 did Garth realize that he wanted to
play country music. "Throughout all the 1980s, I was
a George Strait wannabe," he said.

While music was an interest, sports were a passion,
and Garth often dreamed of becoming a professional
athlete. He played football, basketball, and baseball,

and he was a distance runner on the track team. For three years, he quarterbacked the Millers, the Yukon High School football team. In his sixth game as a senior, however, the coach thought the team would be better served by moving a junior into the quarterback position and Garth to defensive lineman. Though his pride may have been bruised, Garth's enthusiasm for the game and his support of the team never wavered. When his replacement scored the game's winning touchdown, Garth was among the first to rush onto the field to congratulate him.

An above-average student, especially in English, Garth graduated from high school in the spring of 1980. He flirted briefly with the idea of following in his father's footsteps and joining the marines, but Troyal talked him out of it. All the Brooks children were to go to college, his father reminded him. In the fall, Garth followed Kelly to Oklahoma State University (OSU).

When Garth got to college, his passion for sports shifted to music.

The Music Starts

Oklahoma State University is located in Stillwater, just 90 minutes from Yukon. The distance is far enough for a kid to feel the first sense of independence, but close enough to get the laundry done or grab a home-cooked meal. Kelly was in his sophomore year on a track scholarship when Garth became his roommate. The brothers had also shared a room at home. Neither brother smoked or drank. Garth once told his mother, "I could live with Kelly 24 hours a day."

Colleen said neither would try to put anything over on the other. "It wouldn't do either of them any good anyways, because they could see right through each other."

With Garth's less-than-spectacular record as a high school quarterback, he didn't have a chance at playing the position at OSU, and he wasn't big enough to play on the defensive line either. He might have made the baseball team but instead he chose to join the track team and throw the javelin—a light metal spear that is thrown for distance in a track-and-field event. Garth had already developed a strong throwing arm playing football and baseball, so the choice wasn't so unusual. Through constant practice, he steadily improved and even received a partial scholarship.

Athletic excellence again proved elusive, however. His competitors regularly beat Garth's 200-foot javelin throws. One of Garth's biggest disappointments was failing to make the Big Eight Championship Finals during his senior year. Several years later, he was able to look back with a bit more humor, saying, "Threw

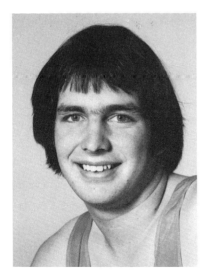

At Oklahoma State University, Garth joined the track team and threw the javelin.

18

the javelin all four years. Stunk all four years. Realized that athletics wasn't going to be my future. Everybody else knew it but me!"

As Garth's dream of a possible sports career evaporated, his love for music continued to grow. He often spent time in his dorm room, playing the guitar and singing. Other students frequently dropped by for impromptu jam sessions that lasted well into the night.

In April 1983, sophomore Garth Brooks was chosen to represent his dormitory in the university's talent contest. He surprised everybody with three Dan Fogelberg songs and won the $50 first prize. Garth's musical reputation began to spread, and he was often asked to sing at campus parties. He also played at Aunt Molly's Rent-Free Music Emporium, another outlet for OSU's amateur musicians. Before long, he was playing for money. Garth's first paying job was at Shotgun Sam's Pizza Parlor in Stillwater.

He was soon playing at Wild Willie's Saloon, a bar popular with OSU students. He earned $100 for a four-hour set. Fans accustomed to seeing Garth in a cowboy hat and jeans might have a hard time recognizing the Garth who played at Wild Willie's. At that time, he had shoulder-length hair, a full beard and mustache, and often wore sweat pants, T-shirt, and a baseball cap. He wasn't making enough money through music to cover all his expenses, so he took another job as a bouncer at Tumbleweed's, a country

While Garth was attending OSU, he played at Willie's Saloon in Stillwater.

western bar and dance club located just outside of Stillwater. A bouncer is someone hired to restrain or remove disorderly people. As big as he was, Garth was still too small to be an effective bouncer. As a result, he was often called on to break up fights between women. In fact, that's how he met his wife, Sandy.

One night he was called to the ladies' room to break up a scuffle. As Garth describes it, he went in and found an attractive blond in tight jeans and a black cowboy hat standing there with her arm stuck in the wall. Another woman was cringing in the corner. When he asked what happened, the blond said, "I missed."

After he freed her arm, he walked her outside and convinced her it was the bar's policy that he escort her home. He called her the next day and asked her for a date. She accepted.

Sandy Mahl graduated from high school in Owasso, Oklahoma, in 1983. She had been a cheerleader, a lifeguard, and had competed briefly as a rodeo rider. Sandy was attending OSU as a child psychology major. She was two years younger than Garth, and she became his first serious female friend.

Sandy describes those early days at Wild Willie's Saloon saying, "He'd just get up and he would play anything from Neil Young to Willie Nelson, Elton John, Billy Joel, or Dan Fogelberg. It was whatever anyone could yell out. He'd say, 'I don't really know that one but I'll try it.' And you would have guys saying, 'No, it's this verse next, and they'd come up and sing along with him on the mike."

Music began to occupy more and more of Garth's time. At one point, he told his parents he wanted to drop out of school to pursue a singing career. He tried to explain to them that he didn't think he'd ever really use a college degree, but they convinced him to finish.

Although Garth struggled with his schoolwork, he graduated in December 1984 with a degree in advertising and marketing. Looking back on his college years, Garth said he regrets not being more serious about his studies while he was there.

Music—both writing it and singing it—became his life. He was good at it, and he knew it. He was playing six nights a week and getting paid for it, and the audiences loved him. The feeling was mutual. By the summer of 1985, he thought he was ready to make his fortune in Nashville.

Garth's first trip to Nashville was unsuccessful.

Nashville Bound

Garth told Sandy about his dream of making it big in Nashville, but he only hinted that he wouldn't be taking her with him. When it came time to leave, he went alone. "I was a jerk. When I left, I didn't tell her, but I wasn't planning on coming back. I didn't think I'd see her again once I moved to Nashville," Garth admits.

When his plans for instant stardom were dashed in Nashville, Garth was too embarrassed to face Sandy or any of his other friends right away. Instead of going back to Stillwater, Garth sought the comfort of his parents' home in Yukon. "He had never really been away from home before, had never been alone," his mother said. "He gets down there and they just shut the door. It wasn't failure. He just didn't know the ins and outs."

Garth needed a few weeks to gain the courage to return to Stillwater and face Sandy. When he did, she welcomed him back. A few months later, he asked her to marry him. She agreed, and on May 24, 1986, they were married.

He got his old day job back at DuPree's sporting goods store, where he had worked for two years while attending OSU. Garth spent his nights singing in Stillwater clubs. He frequently played with the Skinner Brothers, a local classic rock band that occasionally did country music.

In 1986, the Skinner Brothers broke up and regrouped behind Garth as a country band called Santa Fe. Their popularity on the southwestern college circuit grew quickly. Within a year, they were playing at fraternity parties, bars, and clubs from Arizona to Arkansas.

With his confidence restored, Garth planned another trip to Nashville. He was convinced the outcome would be different this time. He wouldn't be going alone—he would be accompanied by his wife and the band.

In the summer of 1987, Garth and Sandy took their $1500 "nest egg" and, with the other band members, rented a five-bedroom house in Hendersonville, near Nashville. But that arrangement didn't last long. Garth described the situation, saying, "You stick five guys, two wives, a kid, a dog, and a cat in one house, and try to see how you deal with the unknown. It was

Garth worked days at DuPree's sporting goods store.

fun for the first month, living with your dreams," he added. "But once again reality rang the doorbell. It just fell apart right in front of our eyes."

Garth and the band had made a pact to stick it out in Nashville for at least six months before anyone could quit and go back to Oklahoma, but they didn't make it. When a record contract failed to materialize, Santa Fe dissolved and the band members went their separate ways. Garth tried everything in his power to keep the band together, and he cried when his efforts failed.

He and Sandy decided to stay in Nashville by themselves. They moved into a three-bedroom apartment, where they lived for the next year. To help make ends meet, Garth got a job as manager of the

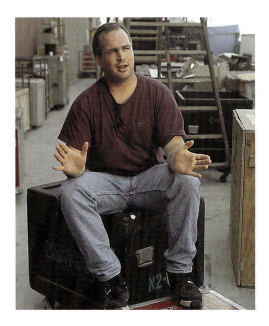

Before getting his break, Garth tried almost every Nashville record company.

Cowtown Boots store in nearby Madison. Sandy worked at temporary clerical jobs. Garth soon exercised his authority as store manager and hired his wife. By working in the store, Sandy could cover for him when he came in late, left early for a meeting, or wanted to hide in the back room to write songs.

Garth knocked on more doors during the following months, trying to sell himself and his music to almost every record company in Nashville. They all turned him down, and familiar feelings of failure and futility began to wash over him once again.

He recalls the time he was driving with Sandy and was crying so hard he had to pull off the road into the parking lot of a fire station. He got out and stood in the pouring rain, beating his head against the roof of the car and yelling at his wife. Sandy screamed back at him to stop.

Later he said, " I thought we weren't going to make it. I thought we were going to crash, trash out, go into debt, poverty, and stuff. It had nothing to do with music. It was two people, newly married, struggling against debt. I thought it was over."

When things settled down, he asked her if they shouldn't just forget the whole thing and move back to Oklahoma. "She sat me down and said, 'Look, I was around when you came back the last time, and I'm not going through that again.'" Sandy consoled Garth, saying, "I think you're good enough and you think you're good enough, so we're going to stay right here."

In November 1987, Garth signed with a new music publishing company, Major Bob Music, headed by Bob Doyle. Doyle soon found some small jobs for Garth. He sang commercial jingles for clients such as Lone Star Beer and John Deere tractors, and he sang on demo tapes for other songwriters. Pam Lewis, a Nashville publicist, joined Doyle, and they became Garth's managers in January 1988. Doyle and Lewis pitched Garth to every major record company in town. All of them, including Capitol Records, turned him down—some more than once.

Garth signed his first record contract after performing at the Bluebird Cafe.

Overnight Success

The Bluebird Cafe is well known in Nashville as a club where new and established artists are given the chance to perform in front of members of the recording industry. One night in May 1988, the Nashville Entertainment Association reserved the club in order to stage its own musical showcase. Doyle took Garth to the Bluebird so Garth could get a firsthand look at his competition.

One of the people scheduled to perform that evening failed to show up, and, when asked, Garth quickly agreed to take his place. Among the many executives in the audience was Lynn Shults of Capitol Records, who had auditioned Garth and turned him down just a few weeks earlier.

Garth sang two songs. When he finished, Shults walked across the room to Garth and Bob Doyle, shook their hands, and said, "You guys got a deal!" Shults explained that the difference between the earlier audition in his office and that night's Bluebird performance was Garth's ability to communicate the passion of his songs to the audience. And the audience was difficult to impress, since it included so many music industry professionals.

Garth signed a contract with Capitol Records on June 17 and received a $10,000 advance, a payment made in advance of future records. He said it was the most money he'd ever had in his life. The advance

Garth began recording his first album in December 1988.

was about the same amount he and Sandy had earned together during the entire previous year. It had taken him only 10 months to get a record contract. Now he had to produce.

By December, Garth began recording his first album. He admits to being scared, but he wanted to make the folks back home proud. Of the album's 10 songs, Garth wrote 5, including "If Tomorrow Never Comes." "This song means a lot to me because of the friends I've lost," he explained. He dedicated it to a former track coach who had died in a 1982 plane crash and to a college roommate killed in a 1985 car accident. The album, titled *Garth Brooks*, was released April 12, 1989. It became the best-selling country album of the 1980s, with sales of more than six million copies.

To help promote the album, Garth formed a new band. He called it Stillwater—as a tribute to his musical roots at OSU. The band toured states throughout the Southwest and Southeast. At the beginning of the tour, even when there were sometimes fewer than 10 people in the audience, Garth and Stillwater played as though they were on stage in front of a stadium full of screaming fans. As the tour continued and more of the album's songs were released as singles, the size and enthusiasm of the crowds grew. "If Tomorrow Never Comes," "The Dance," and "Counting on You" climbed to the top spot on the country

To help promote his album, Garth took his band Stillwater on tour.

music charts, and "Much Too Young to Feel This Damn Old" reached eighth place.

Garth was on the road the entire second half of 1989. He and Sandy spent only 28 days together during that time. Such a long separation would strain even the best relationship, but Sandy began hearing rumors that her husband was being unfaithful. Her fears were confirmed when someone on the tour bus called and told her the rumors were true.

On November 4, Sandy called Garth before a concert and said she was prepared to leave him. She had packed her bags and purchased an airline ticket. "You come home and we'll talk, on my turf, eye to eye," she told him. Garth opened the concert that night in Sikeston, Missouri, with "We Bury the Hatchet."

Later he sang "If Tomorrow Never Comes," a tune Garth had written one night while watching Sandy sleep. Less than a minute into the song, he became choked by tears, and he stopped singing. He told the startled audience how difficult it was to spend so much time on the road and how much he loved his wife. He started over, and this time he was able to finish the song.

Immediately after the concert, Garth flew back to Sandy. He went down on his knees and begged her to forgive him. "He was ashamed, embarrassed, and

An enthusiastic fan gets a hug from Garth.

it was written all over his face," Sandy said. "He had hurt me so bad. I had wasted two years of my life is how I felt." Sandy didn't forgive him right away. She said, "I wanted Garth to feel my pain." But eventually she did forgive him.

"It took a helluva human being to forgive me," he said. "I love her to death. When I've been down, Sandy has given me strength." They both admit it

After he had been unfaithful to his wife, Sandy, Garth begged her forgiveness.

hasn't always been easy, but they work hard at maintaining and improving their relationship, and Sandy now accompanies Garth on tour whenever possible.

His first album peaked at number 2 on *Billboard* magazine's Country Chart and at number 12 on its Top 200 Chart in 1989. Things were beginning to come together, and Garth realized he needed people he could trust around him.

Garth called his brother Kelly and asked him to move to Nashville so they could work together. Kelly had a high level banking position, however, and was reluctant to switch jobs. Besides, Kelly told Garth that he didn't know anything about the music business. Garth called him back and said simply, "I need you." When he heard those words, Kelly promptly gave a 30-day notice to his employer. In April 1990, he joined Garth and Sandy in Nashville to help them manage the money side of the business. Garth also asked his sister to join the band. Betsy accepted and joined Stillwater as a guitarist and background vocalist.

That same April, Garth was nominated for three awards—Top New Male Vocalist, Top Song, and Top Single—at the Academy of Country Music's annual ceremonies. He lost all three, two of them to Clint Black, another newcomer on the country scene.

Garth tips his hat to the audience at the Grand Ole Opry
in October 1991.

Thunder of Controversy Rolls

While no single event can explain Garth's sudden stardom, his first video—"The Dance"—was certainly significant. Music videos have become vital to an album's sales success. While Garth's voice was becoming well known on the nation's airwaves, his face was familiar only to those who had seen him in concert. After the video was released, sales of his first album climbed significantly.

Garth's producer wanted him to do a second album. *No Fences*, released in August 1990, contained the widely popular "Friends in Low Places." Songs such as "The Thunder Rolls," in which a wife shoots her abusive husband, revealed Garth's more serious side.

Meanwhile, in October, Garth's first album was certified platinum, which means that more than one million copies had been sold. Later that month, at the

Country Music Association awards show, Garth received the Horizon Award, presented each year to country music's most promising new artist. He also won the Video of the Year award for "The Dance."

Garth's professional life was gaining momentum. Before the year was over, he had been inducted into the Grand Ole Opry, appeared on NBC's *Tonight Show*, completed his first media tour in London, and ridden in Macy's Thanksgiving Day Parade in New York City.

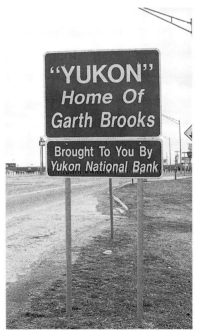

His hometown of Yukon, Oklahoma, shows it's proud of Garth Brooks.

In March 1991, Garth again returned to Yukon though this trip was quite different from the one in 1985. To celebrate Garth's success, his hometown put his name on the water tower, proclaiming Yukon as "The Home of Garth Brooks." A year later, the city also renamed a stretch of State Highway 92 "Garth Brooks Boulevard." He had wanted to make his hometown proud and he had succeeded.

Garth won six awards at the Academy of Country Music gala in April, including Entertainer of the Year, Male Vocalist of the Year, Album of the Year (*No Fences*), and Song of the Year ("The Dance").

Controversy, however, doesn't hide from the famous for long. Garth had filmed a video of "The Thunder Rolls," in which he portrayed the unfaithful husband and wife abuser who is shot at the end of the song as his daughter looks on. Just a week after Garth received the award for his video of "The Dance," The Nashville Network and Country Music Television banned his video of "The Thunder Rolls," saying it was too violent and too graphic. Compared to the sexually exploitive videos of several rock groups and the violence broadcast on television, Garth's video was mild. Besides, Garth argued, his video contained an important message.

Garth was outraged. So was Sandy—but for entirely different reasons. She didn't like the daughter watching the wife shoot the husband, and she didn't appreciate

At the 1991 Academy of Country Music Awards, Garth won six trophies.

the fact that Garth played the role of the unfaithful husband. She protested by refusing to watch the finished video. Nevertheless, controversy spurred sales, and "The Thunder Rolls" became Garth's sixth number one single.

Garth released his third album, *Ropin' the Wind,* in September 1991. It became the first album in history to hold the number one spot on *Billboard* magazine's Top 200 Chart *and* its Country Chart. *Ropin' the Wind* went on to become the second-largest-selling country album of all time—behind *No Fences.* Sales totaled 11 million copies.

In October, Garth once again dominated the Country Music Association ceremonies, capturing awards for Entertainer of the Year, Album of the Year (*No Fences*), Single of the Year ("Friends in Low Places"), and Video of the Year ("The Thunder Rolls").

The pace quickened in 1992. His first television special, "This Is Garth Brooks," aired in January. Twenty-eight million people tuned in to learn more about this man who was making music history. The show—filmed at two sold-out concerts held in the 19,000-seat Reunion Arena in Dallas, Texas—was the highest rated one-hour music special of the season.

Country legend Johnny Cash, *far left,* embraces a tearful Garth Brooks, as Garth accepts his Entertainer of the Year award during the 1992 Country Music Association Awards show. Garth's TV special, *right,* was a huge success.

Sandy appeared with Garth at the 1992 Academy of Country Music Awards.

Later that month, Garth was scheduled to perform at the American Music Awards in Los Angeles, where he would receive awards for Country Male Artist of the Year, Country Single of the Year ("The Thunder Rolls"), and Country Album of the Year (*No Fences*). He and Sandy, who was pregnant with their first baby, arrived the day before the ceremonies.

Shortly after they landed at Los Angeles International Airport, Sandy started suffering stomach pains. Afraid that his wife was having a miscarriage, Garth rushed Sandy into a bathroom and called emergency number 911. She was taken to a nearby hospital where doctors determined that the baby was all right, but they told Sandy to stay off her feet. Garth canceled his performance and promised to stay with Sandy until he was certain both she and the baby were okay. He even spoke publicly about possibly retiring and becoming a full-time dad.

He didn't retire, but he did take some time off to be with his wife. On July 8, 1992, a healthy Taylor Mayne Pearl Brooks was born. She was named for James Taylor (one of Garth's favorite performers), Maine (the

From left to right, publicist and manager Pam Lewis, manager and publisher Bob Doyle (Major Bob Music), Country Music Award's Ed Benson, Garth Brooks, songwriter Kent Blazy, and ASCAP's Connie Bradley appear at a party sponsored by the American Society of Composers, Authors, and Publishers.

state in which she was supposedly conceived), and Minnie Pearl (a legendary Grand Ole Opry star and a friend of the Brookses). Garth was with Sandy for the entire 10 hours she spent in the delivery room. He even cut the baby's umbilical cord. He said he almost cut off the nurse's finger because he was "so dang happy and nervous." Garth took some more time off following Taylor Mayne's birth. He said,"The one gift I want to give this kid is the best gift that my dad and mom ever gave me—attention. . . ."

An aerial view of Garth and Sandy's Goodlettsville, Tennessee, home

Minnie Pearl, a Grand Ole Opry star

Garth and Sandy brought their baby home to a trailer, definitely an odd choice for someone of Garth's new-found wealth. They had recently purchased a 6,000-square-foot home on 20 acres in Goodlettsville, Tennessee, but the house wasn't yet ready, because they were adding another thousand square feet onto the house. Also under construction were a roping arena, racquetball and basketball courts, two sunrooms, a whirlpool, and a nursery.

Beyond the Season, Garth's first Christmas album, was released in August 1992. He donated a portion of the profits from the album to a charity called Feed the Children. The album raised more than $2 million. "This is the most fun I have ever had making an album," Garth said. "I'd make this album every day of my life if I could, because you're singing about what counts."

In September, his fifth album—*The Chase*—was released. Two particular cuts from the album made strong political statements and created another wave of publicity that again helped sales. Garth said he wrote "We Shall Be Free" after the 1992 racial riots in Los Angeles, but he meant the song to be a protest against all forms of injustice and intolerance—including hunger, homelessness, pollution, and discrimination. The song also proclaimed an acceptance of lesbianism and homosexuality, which angered many conservative country music fans. "When we're free to love anyone we choose, then we shall be free," he said in the lyrics. Another song on the album, "Face to Face," dealt with the issue of date rape and encouraged women to have the strength to stand up to men who abuse them.

By the end of 1992, photos of Garth seemed to be everywhere. In addition to the expected coverage by country music magazines, Garth appeared on the covers of *Time, The Saturday Evening Post, People, Entertainment Weekly,* and even *Forbes*—a corporate business magazine. Country music was becoming mainstream due largely to Garth's popularity.

The strain of stardom was beginning to take its toll, however. Garth was trying to balance multiple commitments—tours, appearances, recordings, endorsements, television shows, record contract negotiations, and family. He was at the top of the country music business, but he felt an extraordinary pressure to find a way not only to stay there, but to keep growing. "It's great being on top," Garth said, "but you always have to realize that you can go down that ladder of success just as quickly." He admitted he felt close to breaking.

The 1996 concert in Milwaukee, Wisconsin, sold 55,000 tickets in less than one hour.

Top of the Heap

Perhaps it was the pressure that caused Garth to act like a spoiled star at Super Bowl XXVII in January 1993. Shortly before he was to sing the national anthem, he walked away, angry that NBC refused to show a video he had made. With time running out, the show's producer raced through the crowd looking for a replacement and found the rock group Bon Jovi. Just as the group was about to be introduced, however, NBC found a way to broadcast the video, and Garth sang to his biggest audience ever—over one billion people in 87 countries.

In order to relieve some of the stress that was building up, Garth decided to reorganize some of the commitments in his life. He canceled some and postponed others. Eventually he was able to carve out more time for himself and his family. In addition, he personally renegotiated his record contract to a 20-year deal. Garth pays all the recording costs and receives no money up front, but instead of the low royalties most recording artists receive, he gets almost half of the profits from each album.

Garth soon got the reassurance he wanted that his stardom was not fading. At the Academy of Country Music Awards in May 1993, Garth won his third Entertainer of the Year award—his ninth award from the Academy in just three years. Backstage, he commented on what he'd learned about country music: "It's not rocket science. It's about raising hell and having fun."

And that's exactly what Garth was doing. When *In Pieces,* Garth's sixth album, was released in August 1993, it, too, entered the charts in the number one spot. He said, "We titled this album *In Pieces* because that's pretty much how it came together." He explained that it was more fun to produce because it had more of the feel of a live show.

On January 29, 1994, he performed two concerts at the 36,000-seat Great Western Forum in Los Angeles, California. Tickets for both shows sold out in a record 34 minutes. He sold out the 65,000-seat Texas Stadium in Dallas in 92 minutes. Fans demanded a second show and then a third. Both additional shows sold out in about 90 minutes.

Garth had released six albums in five years. His producers decided he should take a year off before

Garth performed at the Academy of Country Music Awards in 1993.

recording any new material. Instead of albums with new songs, his record company released two albums of songs he had previously recorded. The company issued *The Garth Brooks Collection* and—beginning in September 1994—sold it for a limited time through McDonald's restaurants. Proceeds from this album benefited the Ronald McDonald Children's Charities. The second album, titled *The Hits,* was released in December. The album, a collection of 18 of Garth's best-selling recordings, became the biggest "greatest hits" album in country music sales history. Garth has sold more than 60 million albums, which makes his record sales second only to the Beatles.

Not only his fame but his family, too, continued to grow. On May 3, 1994, Sandy gave birth to their second

Garth and Sandy with their daughter August

daughter, August Anna. Later that month, Garth performed in his second television special, "This Is Garth Brooks, Too." It was a wild show, more like a rock concert than a typical country western performance. Special effects included fire, smoke, and rain, and showcased Garth as the energetic performer that he is.

Garth found that his popularity extended far beyond the shores of the United States. His 1994 world tour played before audiences totaling more than a quarter of a million people in 13 countries. In Spain, fans showed their highest appreciation by shouting *torero* (matador). In Ireland, the press noted that not even Bruce Springsteen, U2, or Bob Dylan had sold so many tickets so quickly. In Australia, a newspaper headline read: "Brooks—Talent Outstrips the Hype."

Before each of Garth's concerts, an announcer tells the crowd to shout and have a good time. At the concert in Rotterdam, Netherlands, however, something apparently got lost in the translation into Dutch. On this particular night the announcer asked the audience to do just the opposite. A somewhat bewildered Garth Brooks walked onstage before an extremely polite and quiet crowd.

Garth's long-awaited seventh album, *Fresh Horses*, was finally released in late 1995. Garth wrote 8 of the album's 10 songs, more than he had written for any other album. He had always said that he wanted no more than half the songs on his albums to be his own. That way, he explained, other songwriters would be encouraged to submit material to him. But he felt most of the songs he'd seen for the album had been off the mark. Also, a "writer's block" that had prevented him from writing songs had finally lifted. "After all the time that we had off, it was like my head finally got cleared enough to start putting pencil to paper again," he said. He wrote the album's last song, "Ireland," for the record number of Irish fans who had attended his concerts. "I really want it to be like a postcard that thanks them," he said.

Before the year ended, plans were underway for yet another world tour. This tour, which took Garth and Stillwater to 77 U.S. cities, began in March 1996. He traveled to Europe in the spring of 1997 then planned to tour Australia before returning to the United States to finish the tour.

Garth took time out in the middle of the tour to return home and be with Sandy when she gave birth to their third child, Allie Colleen, who was born on July 28, 1996. He returned to the tour shortly afterward. His two older daughters, Taylor and August, frequently joined him on the road, but Sandy stayed home to take care of the new baby.

The1996-1998 tour was a project of epic proportions. The show was packed into ten 18-wheelers, carrying 80,000 pounds of sets, lighting, musical equipment, and even Garth's own steel stage. The

At a concert in Dublin, Ireland, *left,* Garth won more fans. Garth—with Sandy—receives his star on Hollywood Boulevard, *right.*

electrical demands of all the gear required Garth to bring his own generators, and it took eight buses to carry the 55 people in the band and crew. The production rivaled the largest and most spectacular rock music shows ever staged.

The tour opened at the Omni Arena in Atlanta, Georgia, on March 13, 1996. When the Atlanta date was announced, fans purchased all 80,000 available tickets within two-and-one-half hours, breaking the auditorium's previous record set by Elvis Presley. That ticket pace was matched in other cities as well. In Phoenix, Arizona, fans bought 53,000 tickets in less than four hours, breaking the city's previous record set by Neil Diamond in 1992. In Auburn Hills, Michigan, more than 90,000 tickets were sold in 90 minutes.

When comparisons are made between Garth and such giant rock and roll and pop stars as Elvis Presley, Billy Joel, the Eagles, and the Beatles, he responds, "I'm scared to death. . . . You can't lie to yourself and say you belong in that club because you're so damned new." And when compared to such legends of country music as Merle Haggard and George Jones, Garth replies, "Those guys are the kings of country to me." He says their music is like collegiate wrestling, and what he does is more like championship wrestling. "We're out there just kinda being silly and stupid, and hopefully the songs are getting across." Most people are not used to this type of humility in their superstars.

Garth speaks to the audience after receiving his award for Favorite Country Male Artist at the American Music Awards in January 1997.

The Man

Garth has lots of help remaining humble. Whenever he returns home to visit his folks, Garth says that the first words out of his father's mouth are always, "You know it's not real, don't you?" Garth tells him that he knows.

Sandy is always there, too. She tolerates crowds of women screaming for her husband, but she occasionally draws the line. She politely but firmly told Garth that people would have more respect for him if he would stop autographing various parts of his female fans' bodies—and he agreed.

The press also has a way of keeping a star's ego in check. *People* magazine named Garth one of the "worst dressed" entertainers in 1993. The article said, "Though John Wayne was his hero, GB looks more Pillsbury Doughboy than big-screen cowboy," adding that he wore shirts "patterned like awnings in Toontown."

Sandy accompanies Garth on tour as much as possible.

Garth has never felt that he had to apologize for his clothes, but comments about his weight (nearly 240 pounds at one point) finally got to him. Someone even made a recording called *Girth Brooks* that included a remake of his song "Thunder Rolls" as "Buttered Rolls." Country star Chris LeDoux once asked Garth if all the talk about his weight bothered him. Garth answered with a lie. "No, it doesn't bother me," he said. He eventually shed 40 pounds, however, and he works hard to keep his weight down.

Garth tries to create as normal an environment as possible for himself, Sandy, and their daughters. "We

Garth's sister, Betsy, *far left,* is a guitarist and background vocalist in his band.

continually surround them [the children] with people that we grew up with, so hopefully they can get a look at what real life is," he said. Of course that includes Garth's sister and brother who both work with him.

"I'm so glad Kelly and Betsy are on the road with Garth," his father said. "The old nails that were put in his shoes keep him level, because he can talk to them as his brother and sister. They are not strictly business." And road manager Mick Weber is Garth's friend from the second grade.

The value of keeping family members around can be seen in his sister's comments: "I can't see him myself as a sex symbol, but a lot of people do. I laugh, but that's what sisters are for I think!" She added with a smile, "I've never seen anything grow as fast as Garth—besides fungus!"

Garth never seems to forget his roots and the people who have helped him along the way. Read the liner notes from his albums and you'll see Garth thanking everyone from his producer to his truck drivers to the makers of his cowboy hats, jeans, boots, and even to the folks at DuPree Sports back in Stillwater. The notes from *Fresh Horses* also included a

Garth asked country music radio stations to observe the first anniversary of the bombing of the federal building in Oklahoma City on April 19. The bombing took place in 1995.

repeat proposal: "Sandy, will you marry me? Taylor and August, you're my reason why."

Garth also holds his fans in high regard. He knows it all started—and could end—with them. Despite the fact that he could charge just about any price he wanted for his concert tickets, he has kept the price at or below $20 throughout his career—about half of what other major acts charge.

When asked about the prices of tickets for his own concerts, Garth quips, "I've seen the show, and it ain't worth it." Then he adds, "Hopefully, more people can come see us if we keep ticket prices down." While this approach is probably sincere and makes good public relations sense, there is more. Low ticket prices also mean people have money left over to buy T-shirts and other concert souvenirs.

Before each performance in a new arena, Garth says he climbs to the farthest seat to see what the stage looks like from there. "I look down there and I try and start figuring out ways how I am going to make this person in this seat somehow feel special."

He has another way of making people feel special, too. He often reserves seats in the first few rows. Shortly before the concert begins, members of his crew climb to the top rows of the arena and select people to sit in the front seats.

Early in his career, a Garth Brooks fan club was started. For the $10 dues, members got a chance to go backstage and talk with Garth after his performances. Due to his rapidly increasing popularity, however, this practice became impossible. Garth asked fan club president Tami Rose to return everyone's money. In place of the club, fans can subscribe to a quarterly magazine about Garth for $5 a year. Because his fans stuck with him, the magazine is called *the believer.*

At the American Music Awards in January 1996, Garth gave yet another sign that he had a firm grasp on reality. First, he brought the audience to tears by singing "The Change" in front of video scenes from the 1995 Oklahoma City bombing. Later that evening, he won all the awards for which he was nominated: Country Male Artist of the Year, Overall Artist of the Year, and Country Album of the Year. Garth then stunned the audience by leaving the last award at the podium. He said later that he didn't deserve to receive it for a collection of past hits. Instead, he felt it should have gone to a group called Hootie and the Blowfish, whose sales Garth credited with keeping a lot of record retailers alive in 1995.

The pace for Garth shows no signs of slowing down—and won't, if he has anything to say about it. He has commented, "It's like never relax, never take that breath, never stop to get that drink of water. You can always smell the roses when you're running with them in your hand." He expresses concern about being better known for what he's done than what he's

Garth and Sandy attend the 1996 American Music Awards show, *below.* Garth waves his hat after accepting the award for Favorite Male Musical Performer at the 1997 People's Choice Awards show, *right.*

doing. It's that reluctance to stand on past accomplishments that drives Garth.

At the end of his first concert-length video, Garth wrote a note saying, "I feel as if I'm a child again, watching an Oklahoma thunderstorm gathering in the distance, anticipating its wonder yet fearing its potential . . . and loving every minute of it."

He appears to be doing just that.

ABOUT THE AUTHOR

Paul M. Howey is a freelance writer and photographer. A long-time country music fan, he lives in Chandler, Arizona, and enjoys hiking in the desert and climbing the nearby mountains.

ACKNOWLEDGMENTS

Archive Photos/Lee, 8; Archives of Music City News, 43; AP/Wide World Photos, 34, 36, 40, 41 (left), 48, 51, 56, 60, 63 (right); © John Barrett/Globe Photos, Inc., 44; The Bluebird Cafe, 28; © Michael Ferguson/Globe Photos, Inc., 52; © Beth Gwinn/Globe Photos, Inc., 14; © Stephen Holman, 20, 25; London Features International/Ron Wolfson, 1, 16, 26, 33, 45, 58; London Features International/Gregg De Guire, 22; Music City News, 43; © Kyran O'Brien/Globe Photos, Inc., 54 (left); Oklahoma State University, Department of Athletics, 18; Photofest, 2; © Van Redin/Globe Photos, Inc., 41 (right); © Hugh Scott, 11, 30, 32, 38 (both), 59; Seth Poppel Yearbook Archives, 10, 12; © Vincent Zuffante/Star File, Inc., 42, 54 (right), 63 (left).

Front and back cover photos © Dave Benett/Globe Photos, Inc.

Frances Harper Junior High School
4000 East Covell Blvd.
Davis, CA 95618